MARK HAYES

Glory, Honor and Praise

Arrangements for Piano

Products Available
Piano Book 0-6330-1495-8
Listening Cassette 0-6330-1522-9
Listening CD 0-6330-1527-X

GENEVOX

ISBN 0-6330-1495-8

© Copyright 2000 GENEVOX, Nashville, TN 37234.
Possession of a CCLI license does not grant you permission to make copies of this piece of music.
For clarification about the rights CCLI does grant you, please call 1-800-234-2446.

Foreword

For the last twenty years I have played for morning worship at least a couple of Sundays each month at my home church in Kansas City as a volunteer. Through that experience and my travels to other churches around the country, I became somewhat of a student of worship. As I played, I learned so much by watching the faces of my congregation as they sang hymns and contemporary worship songs. I adapted as our church moved from traditional to contemporary and back to a more blended worship style. No matter what style or what type of music we choose, the members of my church, like many others, love to sing. They love to worship corporately.

Through the years I have become more and more aware of the power of instrumental music when it is played with artistry and care. Just a simple praise chorus, when played with sensitivity to the Spirit has the potential to connect people with God in a way that words cannot.

Since that time, I have arranged solo piano music that reflects those experiences, and the response has been overwhelmingly positive. I have chosen some of my favorite praise and worship songs and combined them with familiar hymns for this newest collection, "Glory, Honor and Praise."

My hope is that you will find the same joy and potential for worship that I have found in these songs as you practice and perform them. Find a quiet time and space to play through these songs the first time. Get to know the beauty of this music and then share it with anyone and everyone who needs a touch of God's Spirit in their lives.

Mark Hayes

Contents

Blest Be the Tie That Binds Us Together 55

El Shaddai 60

Here I Am, Lord 26

How Beautiful 20

I Worship You, Almighty God
  with Holy, Holy, Holy 38

Let There Be Glory and Honor and Praises
  with To God Be the Glory 9

On Eagle's Wings 44

Rock of My Salvation 14

Servant Medley
  with The Servant Song
  and Make Me a Servant 65

Shout to the Lord 49

This Is the Day to Rejoice Medley
  with Rejoice in the Lord Always
  and What a Mighty God We Serve
  and This Is the Day 70

Worthy of Worship 32

Let There Be Glory and Honor and Praises

Let there be glory and honor and praises;
Glory and honor to Jesus.
Glory and honor,
Glory and honor to Him.

Words and Music by James and Elizabeth Greenelsh

© Copyright 1978 Integrity's Hosanna! Music.
c/o Integrity Incorporated, 1000 Cody Road, Mobile, Al 36695.
All rights reserved. International copyright secured.
Used by permission.

To God Be the Glory

To God be the glory, great things He hath done;
So loved He the world that He gave us His Son,
Who yielded His life an atonement for sin,
And opened the lifegate that all may go in.

O perfect redemption, the purchase of blood,
To every believer the promise of God;
The vilest offender who truly believes,
That moment from Jesus a pardon receives.

Great things He hath taught us,
great things He hath done,
And great our rejoicing through Jesus the Son;
But purer, and higher, and greater will be
Our wonder, our victory, when Jesus we see.

Praise the Lord, praise the Lord,
Let the earth hear His voice!
Praise the Lord, praise the Lord,
Let the people rejoice!
O come to the Father, through Jesus the Son,
And give Him the glory, great things He hath done.

Words by Fanny J. Crosby
Music by William H. Doane

Rock of My Salvation

You are the Rock of my salvation,
You are the strength of my life.
You are my hope and my inspiration,
Lord, unto You will I cry.
I believe in You, believe in You,
For Your faithful love to me.
You have been my help in time of need;
Lord, unto You will I cleave.
You are the Rock of my salvation,
Your are the strength of my life.

Words and Music by Teresa Muller

© Copyright 1982 by Maranatha! Music.
All rights reserved. Used by permission.

How Beautiful

How beautiful the hands that served
the wine and the bread
and the sons of the earth.
How beautiful the feet that walked
the long dusty roads and the hill to the cross.

How beautiful, how beautiful,
how beautiful is the body of Christ.

How beautiful the heart that bled,
that took all my sin and bore it instead.
How beautiful the tender eyes
that choose to forgive and never despise.

How beautiful, how beautiful,
how beautiful is the body of Christ.

And as He laid down His life,
we offer this sacrifice — that we will live
just as He died: Willing to pay the price,
willing to pay the price.

How beautiful the radiant Bride
who waits for her Groom with His light in her eyes.
How beautiful when humble hearts give
the fruit of pure lives so that others may live.

How beautiful, how beautiful,
how beautiful is the body of Christ.

How beautiful the feet that bring
the sound of good news and the love of the King.
How beautiful the hands that serve
the wine and the bread and the sons of the earth.

How beautiful, how beautiful,
how beautiful is the body of Christ.

Words and Music by Twila Paris

© Copyright 1990 Ariose Music/ASCAP, a division of
Star Song Communications and Mountain Spring Music/ASCAP.
Adm. by Gaither Copyright Management. All rights reserved.
International copyright secured. Used by permission.

Here I Am, Lord

I, the Lord of sea and sky,
I have heard My people cry.
All who dwell in deepest sin
My hand will save.
I who made the stars of night,
I will make their darkness bright.
Who will bear My light to them?
Whom shall I send?

I, the Lord of snow and rain,
I have borne My people's pain.
I have wept for love of them,
They turn away.
I will break their hearts of stone,
Give them hearts for love alone.
I will speak My word to them.
Whom shall I send?

I, the Lord of wind and flame,
I will tend the poor and lame.
I will set a feast for them,
My hand will save.
Finest bread I will provide
Till their hearts be satisfied.
I will give My life to them.
Whom shall I send!

Here I am, Lord.
Is it I, Lord?
I have heard You calling in the night.
I will go, Lord,
If You lead me.
I will hold Your people in my heart.

Words and Music by Daniel L. Schutte
Based on Isaiah 6:8

© Copyright 1981 by Daniel L. Schutte and New Dawn Music,
5536 NE Hassalo, Porland, OR 97213.
All rights reserved. Used by permission.

Worthy of Worship

Worthy of worship, worthy of praise,
worthy of honor and glory;
Worthy of all the glad songs we can sing,
worthy of all of the offerings we bring.

Worthy of reverence, worthy of fear,
worthy of love and devotion;
Worthy of bowing and bending of knees,
worthy of all this and added to these...

Almighty Father, Master and Lord,
King of all kings and Redeemer,
Wonderful Counselor, Comforter, Friend,
Savior and Source of our life without end.

You are worthy, Father, Creator.
You are worthy, Savior, Sustainer.
You are worthy, worthy and wonderful;
Worthy of worship and praise.

Words by Terry W. York
Music by Mark Blankenship

Music © Copyright 1988 McKinney Music, Inc. (BMI).
Words © Copyright 1988 Van Ness Press, Inc. (ASCAP).
All rights reserved.

I Worship You, Almighty God

I worship You, Almighty God,
There is none like You.
I worship You, O Prince of Peace,
That is what I want to do.
I give You praise,
For You are my righteousness.
I worship You, Almighty God,
There is none like You.

Words and Music by Sondra Corbett-Wood

© Copyright 1983 Integrity's Hosanna! Music.
c/o Integrity Incorporated, 1000 Cody Road, Mobile, AL 36695.
All rights reserved. International copyright secured.
Used by permission.

Holy, Holy, Holy

Holy, holy, holy! Lord God Almighty!
Early in the morning our song shall rise to Thee;
Holy, holy, holy, merciful and mighty!
God in three Persons, blessed Trinity!

Holy, holy, holy! all the saints adore Thee,
Casting down their golden crowns
around the glassy sea;
Cherubim and seraphim falling down before Thee,
Who wert, and art, and evermore shalt be.

Holy, holy, holy! though the darkness hide Thee,
Though the eye of sinful man Thy glory may not see;
Only Thou art holy; there is none beside Thee,
Perfect in power, in love, and purity.

Holy, holy, holy! Lord God Almighty!
All Thy works shall praise Thy name,
in earth, and sky, and sea;
Holy, holy, holy; merciful and mighty!
God in three Persons, blessed Trinity!

Words by Reginald Heber
Music by John B. Dykes

On Eagle's Wings

And God will raise you up on eagle's wings,
Bear you on the breath of dawn,
Make you to shine as the sun,
And hold you in the palm of His hand.

Words and Music by Michael Joncas
Adapted from Psalm 91

© Copyright 1979, 1991 New Dawn Music,
5536 NE Hassalo, Portland, OR 97213.
All rights reserved. Used by permission.

Shout to the Lord

My Jesus, My Savior,
Lord, there is none like You,
All of my days, I want to praise
The wonders of Your mighty love.
My comfort, my shelter,
Tower of refuge and strength,
Let every breath, all that I am
Never cease to worship You.

Shout to the Lord,
All the earth let us sing
Power and majesty,
Praise to the King.
Mountains bow down
And the seas will roar
At the sound of Your name.
I sing for joy
At the work of Your hands.
Forever I'll love You,
Forever I'll stand.
Nothing compares to the promise
I have in You.

Words and Music by Darlene Zschech

© Copyright 1993 Darlene Zschech/Hillsong Publishing
(adm. in U.S. & Canada by Integrity's Hosanna! Music).
c/o Integrity Incorporated, 1000 Cody Road, Mobile, AL 36695.
All rights reserved. International copyright secured.
Used by permission.

Bind Us Together

Bind us together, Lord;
Bind us together
with cords that cannot be broken.
Bind us together, Lord;
Bind us together, Lord;
Bind us together with love.

There is only one God,
There is only one King,
There is only one body;
That is why we can sing.

Made for the glory of God,
Purchased by His precious Son.
Born with the right to be clean,
For Jesus the victory has won.

You are the family of God,
You are the promise divine.
You are God's chosen desire,
You are the glorious new wine.

Words and Music by Bob Gillman

© Copyright 1977 by Kingsway's Thank You Music.
All rights reserved. Used by permission.

Blest Be the Tie

Blest be the tie that binds
Our hearts in Christian love;
The fellowship of kindred minds
Is like to that above.

Before our Father's throne
We pour our ardent prayers;
Our fears, our hopes, our aims are one,
Our comforts and our cares.

We share our mutual woes,
Our mutual burdens bear;
And often for each other flows
The sympathizing tear.

When we asunder part,
It gives us inward pain;
But we shall still be joined in heart,
And hope to meet again.

Words by John Fawcett
Music by Johann G. Nägeli

El Shaddai

Through Your love and through the ram,
You saved the Son of Abraham;
Through the power of Your hand,
You turned the sea into dry land.
To the outcast on her knees,
You were the God who really sees;
And by Your might,
You set Your children free.

Through the years You made it clear
That the time of Christ was near;
Though the people couldn't see
What Messiah ought to be.
Though Your Word contained the plan,
They just could not understand
Your most awesome work was done
Through the frailty of Your Son.

El Shaddai, El Shaddai,
El Elyonna Adonai.
Age to age, You're still the same
By the power of the Name.
El Shaddai, El Shaddai
Erkamkana Adonai.
We will praise and lift You high,
El Shaddai.

Words and Music by
John W. Thompson and Michael Card

© Copyright 1981 Whole Armor Publishing Co. (ASCAP).
All rights reserved. Used by permission.

The Servant Song

We are travelers on a journey,
Fellow pilgrims on the road;
We are here to help each other
Walk the mile and bear the load.
I will hold the Christ-light for you
In the nighttime of your fear;
I will hold my hand out to you,
Speak the peace you long to hear.

Sister, let me be your servant,
Let me be as Christ to you;
Pray that I may have the grace to
Let you be my servant, too.
Brother, let me be your servant,
Let me be as Christ to you;
Pray that I may have the grace to
Let you be my servant, too.

I will weep when you are weeping,
When you laugh, I'll laugh with you;
I will share your joy and sorrow,
Till we've seen this journey through.
When we sing to God in heaven,
We shall find such harmony,
Born of all we've known together
Of Christ's love and agony.

Words by Richard Gillard
Music from *The Sacred Harp*, 1844

© Copyright 1977 Scripture in Song (a div. of Integrity Music, Inc.).
c/o Integrity Incorporated, 1000 Cody Road, Mobile, AL 36695.
All rights reserved. International copyright secured.
Used by permission.

Make Me a Servant

Make me a servant, humble and meek;
Lord, let me lift up those who are weak.
And may the prayer of my heart always be:
Make me a servant, make me a servant,
Make me a servant today.

Words and Music by Kelly Willard

© Copyright 1982 by Maranatha! Music and Willing Heart Music.
All rights reserved. Used by permission.

Rejoice in the Lord Always

Rejoice in the Lord always:
 again I say, Rejoice.
Rejoice in the Lord always:
 again I say, Rejoice.

Rejoice, rejoice,
And again I say, Rejoice.
Rejoice, rejoice,
And again I say Rejoice.

Rejoice in the Lord always:
 again I say, Rejoice.
Rejoice in the Lord always:
 again I say, Rejoice.

Words from Philippians 4:4
Music, Unknown

What a Mighty God We Serve

What a mighty God we serve,
What a mighty God we serve;
Angels bow before Him,
Heaven and earth adore Him,
What mighty God we serve.

Words, Anonymous
Music, Anonymous

This Is the Day

This is the day, this is the day
 that the Lord hath made,
 that the Lord hath made.
We will rejoice, we will rejoice
and be glad in it, and be glad in it.
This is the day that the Lord hath made;
We will rejoice and be glad in it.
This is the day, this is the day
 that the Lord hath made.

Words and Music by Les Garrett

© Copyright 1967, 1980 Scripture In Song.
Admin. by Maranatha! Music.
All rights reserved. Used by permission.

Let There Be Glory and Honor and Praises
with To God Be the Glory

Words and Music by
JAMES and ELIZABETH GREENELSH
Arranged by Mark Hayes

© Copyright 1978 and this arr. © Copyright 2001 Integrity's Hosanna! Music.
c/o Integrity Incorporated, 1000 Cody Road, Mobile, AL 36695.
All rights reserved. International copyright secured. Used by permission.

*"To God Be the Glory," Music by William H. Doane.
Let There Be Glory and Honor and Praises — 3

Rock of My Salvation

Words and Music by
TERESA MULLER
Arranged by Mark Hayes

© Copyright 1982 and this arr. © Copyright 2001 by Maranatha! Music.
All rights reserved. Used by permission.

(no pedal, articulate well)
Rock of My Salvation — 3

Rock of My Salvation — 5

How Beautiful

Words and Music by
TWILA PARIS
Arranged by Mark Hayes

© Copyright 1990 and this arr. © Copyright 2001 by Ariose Music (a div. of StarSong)/ASCAP
and Mountain Spring Music/ASCAP. Adm. by EMI Christian Music Group.
All rights reserved. Used by permission.

Here I Am, Lord

DANIEL L. SCHUTTE
Arranged by Mark Hayes

© Copyright 1981 and this arr. © Copyright 2001 Daniel L. Schutte and New Dawn Music,
5536 NE Hassalo, Portland, OR 97213.
All rights reserved. Used by permission.

Here I Am, Lord — 6

Worthy of Worship
Judson

MARK BLANKENSHIP
Arranged by Mark Hayes

Moderately, with great expression ($\quarternote$ = ca. 88)

Music Copyright © 1988 McKinney Music, Inc. (BMI).
This arr. © Copyright 2001 McKinney Music, Inc. (BMI) in *Glory, Honor and Praise*.
All rights reserved. Nashville, TN 37234.

Worthy of Worship — 6

I Worship You, Almighty God

with Holy, Holy, Holy

Words and Music by
SONDRA CORBETT-WOOD
Arranged by Mark Hayes

© Copyright 1983 and this arr. © Copyright 2001 Integrity's Hosanna! Music/ASCAP.
c/o Integrity Incorporated, 1000 Cody Road, Mobile, AL 36695.
All rights reserved. Used by permission.

I Worship You, Almighty God — 2

*"Holy, Holy, Holy," Tune NICAEA by John B. Dykes.

I Worship You, Almighty God — 3

On Eagle's Wings

MICHAEL JONCAS
Arranged by Mark Hayes

© Copyright 1979, 1991, and this arr. © Copyright 2001 New Dawn Music,
5536 NE Hassalo, Portland, OR 97213.
All rights reserved. Used by permission.

On Eagle's Wings — 3

On Eagle's Wings — 4

Shout to the Lord

Words and Music by
DARLENE ZSCHECH
Arranged by Mark Hayes

© Copyright 1993 and this arr. © Copyright 2001 Darlene Zschech/Hillsong Publishing
(Adm. in U.S. & Canada by Integrity's Hosanna! Music).
c/o Integrity Incorporated, 1000 Cody Road, Mobile, AL 36695.
All rights reserved. International copyright secured. Used by permission.

Shout to the Lord — 3

Blest Be the Tie That Binds Us Together

BOB GILLMAN
Arranged by Mark Hayes

*"Blest Be the Tie," Tune DENNIS by Johann G. Nägeli.

© Copyright 1977 and this arr. © Copyright 2001 by Kingsway's Thank You Music.
All rights reserved. Used by permission.

Blest Be the Tie That Binds Us Together — 3

Blest Be the Tie That Binds Us Together — 4

El Shaddai

JOHN THOMPSON
Arranged by Mark Hayes

© Copyright 1981 and this arr. © Copyright 2001 Whole Armor Publishing Co. (ASCAP).
All rights reserved. Used by permission.

Servant Medley

The Servant Song
Make Me a Servant

Arranged by Mark Hayes

*"The Servant Song," Tune BEACH SPRING from *The Sacred Harp*, 1844.

© Copyright 1977 and this arr. © Copyright 2001 Scripture In Song (a div. of Integrity Music, Inc.).
c/o Integrity Incorporated, 1000 Cody Road, Mobile, Al 36695.
All rights reserved. International copyright secured. Used by permission.

Servant Medley — 2

*"Make Me a Servant," Words and Music by Kelly Willard. © Copyright 1982 by Maranatha! Music and Willing Heart Music. All rights reserved. Used by permission.

Servant Medley — 3

This Is the Day to Rejoice Medley

Rejoice in the Lord Always
What a Mighty God We Serve
This Is the Day

Arranged by Mark Hayes

*"Rejoice in the Lord Always," Source Unknown.

© Copyright 2001 Van Ness Press, Inc. (ASCAP) in *Glory, Honor and Praise*.
Nashville, TN 37234.

*"What a Mighty God We Serve," Source Unknown.

*"This Is the Day," Words and Music by Les Garrett. © Copyright 1967, 1980 Scripture In Song.
Admin. by Maranatha! Music. All rights reserved. Used by permission.
This Is the Day to Rejoice Medley — 4

This Is the Day to Rejoice Medley — 6

This Is the Day to Rejoice Medley — 7